POO or FALSE?

A COMPLETELY CRAPPY QUIZ BOOK

POO OR FALSE?

A COMPLETELY CRAPPY QUIZ BOOK

HEADLINE

First published in 2019
by HEADLINE PUBLISHING GROUP

1

Cataloguing in Publication Data is available from the British Library

Hardback ISBN 978 1 4722 6 976 8

Designed by Beau Merchant at Toy Soldier Creative

Printed and bound in Great Britain by Clays Ltd, Elcograf S.p.A

HEADLINE PUBLISHING GROUP
An Hachette UK Company
Carmelite House
50 Victoria Embankment
London
EC4Y 0DZ

www.headline.co.uk
www.hachette.co.uk

'I'd give it five minutes if I were you.'

- Florence Nightingale

HELLO READER!

Welcome to *Poo or False?* The completely crappy quiz book the world has been crying out for! Its aim is to be both educational and to examine the human condition on a deeply philosophical level. Ahem. There are a few likely scenarios where you'll have found yourself picking up this book and flicking to this very page. Let's run through them, shall we?

1. Christmas Day, 10:30am

The morning dead zone. The giddiness of Santa's arrival and his bulging sack (stop sniggering at the back) has passed. The turkey's still a few hours off. You've got about half an hour before it's technically acceptable to start drinking. You've opened your Terry's Chocolate Orange and a pair of those gloves you can heat up in the microwave. But what's this? You shake the parcel. 'It's a book!' you say, dutifully following UK law. And now you're reading this page, and now you're going to do this quiz about poo, and it turns out you started drinking an hour ago, and isn't Christmas brilliant?

1

2. Christmas Day, 4:30pm

The afternoon dead zone. The post-lunch slump. Relatives lie snoozing around you like winter wasps hammered on fermented apple. Days seem to have passed. You are simultaneously incredibly full and yet capable of eating an entire ham, pebble-dashed with Quality Street.

Decent telly doesn't start for another couple of hours.

But what's this? Oh yes, it's the stocking-filler toilet book your brother-in-law got you! And now you're reading these words! Come on, a quick round of this crappy quiz and then you're onto the 5pm Baileys. It's textbook stuff.

3. Any office Christmas party, December 1st–December 20th, 5:20pm – 7:50pm

Mike from head office bought you this for secret santa, and fair play actually, because you wouldn't think him capable of having a sense of humour, because he rides one of those little portable scooters into work and cooks haddock in the microwave in the shared kitchen. Wait, hang on, what's happening? No, don't go! Don't you dare leave me, this book, in this pub next to the mugs with 'keep calm and carry on Marketing!' on them.

Damn you to hell . . .

. . . Oh, you were just going to the toilet. Fair enough. That neatly brings us on to . . .

The Rules

This vital, important tome contains 100 questions on the mighty matter of poo. Some are a simple matter of deciding whether something is poo or false, others require you to choose the one true poo out of three.

You can find the answers on page 123. OK, got it? Well, what are you waiting for?

Get crapping!

1

In 2015, a British Airways flight had to be turned around, but why?

A: Someone onboard had a poo so toxic that it had to turn around and land after just 30 minutes.

B: A passenger called Suzy Shitts became unruly after air stewards repeatedly mocked her name.

C: The captain soiled himself and was too embarrassed to admit it, so pretended the smell was coming from an electrical failure.

2

The military has a history with poo. But which of these is true?

A: In 2003, an American reconnaissance plane in Iraq captured an image of a twenty-foot wide drawing in the dirt showing George Bush getting crapped on by Saddam Hussein. The site was then bombed.

B: Stalin had a secret lab to analyse the faeces of other foreign leaders for the purpose of constructing psychological portraits.

C: In World War One, the French Army investigated the possibility of 'poo dynamite' – a system where soldiers could weaponise their poo by attaching a charge to stools and hurling them into German trenches.

3

Poo or false?

Neil Armstrong left behind four bags of poo on the moon.

A: Poo

B: False

4

Poo or false?

When researcher Tilda March discovered a new species of tree frog in Ecuador in January 2019, her daughter suggested she name it Pooey McPooface, but she was voted down by colleagues 7-6.

A: Poo

B: False

5

Which of these beach-based poo facts is the true poo?

A: Some faeces that appeared overnight on Brighton Pier caused such distress that the police were called and the pier was shut down for over eight hours.

B: The parrotfish eats dead coral and then poos out sand, which is what all the 'white sandy' beaches in Hawaii are made up of.

C: Like all crabs, the Jonah crab, native to North America, walks sideways. But it is the only known species to have been observed walking forwards, which it does when it is preparing to defecate.

6

Poo or false?

In Japan, they have an expression (Mariko Aoki) to describe the sudden urge to poo when you're in a book shop.

A: Poo

B: False

7

Which of these animal facts is the true poo?

A: Male dung beetles will fashion delightful poo sculptures in order to attract females.

B: Male flying squirrels will chuck balls of poo down at perspective mates to attract their attention.

C: Male hippos fling their poo by twirling their tails in order to impress females and mark their territory.

8

Which one of these Samuel Pepys quotes is real, and therefore the true poo?

A: '...and going down into my cellar to look, I put my foot into a great heap of turds, by which I find that Mr Turner's house of office is full and comes into my cellar, which doth trouble me...'.

B: '...I took a great mound of shitt in my palm and did fling it mercilessly at the young lad, who yelped and took off at quite a pace.'

C: '...but upon waking I found that in my drunken stupor I had contrived to befoul the bed, the awful muck spread around the sheets and valance, to my somewhat considerable shame.'

If the daily output of London's pooers was collected, how far would it reach?

A: 230km

B: 800km

C: 3,300km

10

Which one of these was a real job in Victorian London?

A: 'Pure collectors'. Pure collectors would search the streets for canine crap, then cart it to south London where it was bought by tanners, who used the poo to help purify the leather they made and sold.

B: 'Old Muckers'. As the popularity of circuses and freak shows grew, so did the disgusting practice of throwing turds at criminals in the stocks. Muckers would collect the poo from the streets and provide it to the stocks owners for a measly price.

C: 'Sweepers'. Prominent gentlemen wishing to court women by walking them down a stretch of London's streets or along the Thames bank would employ sweepers to remove turds from the pavement in order to make the experience more pleasant for the ladies.

'I have nothing to declare but my genius. And that I just did a massive blog on that plane.'

—Oscar Wilde

'I have nothing to declare but my genius. And that I just did a massive plop on that plane'

- Oscar Wilde

11

Which one of these poo-based methods of killing is the true poo?

A: A famous Persian assassin's preferred method of killing was to hide in latrines underneath toilets and stab their target from below.

B: Scythians, a central Eurasian nomadic people, would use poisoned arrows tainted with their own shit, which would cause infections in their victims if the arrow itself didn't kill them.

C: Aradic, former 'advisor' to Attila the Hun, and King of the Gepids, advocated the tactic of his soldiers balling up fistfuls of their own shit, filled with stones and thorns, and hurling them from hidden aerial positions at would-be attackers.

12

Which of these is a tale of true poo heroism?

A: The Canadian tribesman who shat into his hand, waited for the shit to freeze, fashioned it into a blade and slaughtered a dog, using its skin for warmth, its meat for food, and its rib cage for a crude sledge.

B: The Austrian hunter who was attacked by a wolf and survived by drowning the animal in a puddle filled with his own diarrhoea.

C: The Icelandic warrior who buried himself in a mound of bird shit in order to keep warm until the ice sheet he was floating on got close enough to dry land.

13

When it comes to the battle of the sexes, even poo makes an appearance. According to medical studies, who technically has a harder job pooing?

A: Men, because on average they have tighter rectums.

B: Women, because they have longer colons.

C: Neither is actually true.

14

Which of these statements concerning the ideal stool sample is the true poo?

A: Healthy poo floats.

B: Healthy poo sinks.

C: Healthy poo bobs up and down.

15

Which of these is the true poo origin of the word 'shit'?

A: Cow pats were used as fuel on ships in the 1800s, but because of the dangers of them exploding due to methane reacting to candle flames, they were kept high up on the ship, away from the lower holds. Thus, the boxes containing them were marked: SHIP HIGH IN TRANSIT, which was eventually just shortened to SHIT.

B: It is derived from the word scite, from the 14th century, meaning 'dung'.

C: It is an onomatopoeic term first noted down by Ceolfrith, a contemporary of the Venerable Bede, to describe the noise of his farts.

16

Which of these is the true poo origin of the word 'crap'?

A: It comes from Thomas Crapper, the inventor of the flushing toilet.

B: It is a mixture of the Dutch world krappen, 'to pluck off', and the French word crappe 'rejected matter'.

C: It came from the gambling game 'craps', itself an American derivation of the word 'crabs' (the original English name for the game).

17

Which of these true poo chaps invented the flushing toilet?

A: Thomas Crapper

B: Lord James Jameson

C: Sir John Harrington

18

Texts dating back to 1850 BCE record Ancient Egyptians using crocodile poop as a form of which true poo?

A: Contraception

B: Ammunition

C: Wall building material

19

Poo or false?

Your poo is full of valuable metals such as silver and gold.

A: Poo

B: False

20

Poo or false?

Nazi troops in Africa believed driving over camel poop with their tanks was good luck. The Allies, therefore, decided to disguise landmines with camel poop to blow up their tanks.

A: Poo

B: False

'Look at him, walking around like his shit doesn't stink'

- Mother Teresa

21

Poo or false?

In London, the first bus running exclusively on human poo and household waste debuted with a 15 mile route, 4 days a week.

A: Poo

B: False

22

Poo or false?

In upstate New York in 2016, a pile of horse feces got so hot it spontaneously caught fire, taking three fire departments two hours to totally extinguish the flames.

A: Poo

B: False

23

Poo or false?

The world's tallest skyscraper in Dubai doesn't have a sewage system. Instead, all of its poop is driven away in trucks to a sewage facility.

A: Poo

B: False

24

Poo or false?

George Clooney supposedly played a practical joke on his roommate by cleaning out his cat's litter box and defecating in it, to make his roommate think his cat had some serious poo problems.

A: Poo

B: False

25

Poo or false?

In rare cases of severe constipation, people reportedly have suffered from 'faecal vomiting.' When the poo can't exit through the anus, it forces matter from the small intestine to shoot up and out of a person's mouth.

A: Poo

B: False

Poo or false?

The phrase 'do bears shit in the woods?'
was reportedly invented by
Charles Darwin.

A: Poo

B: False

27

When was the phrase 'Shit happens' first recorded as being used?

A: 1888

B: 1939

C: 1964

28

Scientists were monitoring whale stress levels by analysing their poo and found that their stress dropped immediately following the 9/11 attacks. But why was it?

A: All air traffic was halted, which calmed the oceans of low frequency noise, helping the whales communicate more easily.

B: The noise from the attacks drove away opportunist sharks that occasionally attack whales.

C: The vibrations from the attacks sent whales to calmer waters that they wouldn't usually go to.

29

Poo or false?

Sloths only poo once a week, something scientists call 'the poo dance'.

A: Poo

B: False

30

What shape is Wombat crap?

A: Perfectly spherical

B: Triangular

C: Cubic

'Life is what happens when you're
busy making other plans.'

— John Lennon

'Life is what happens when you're busy making other plans.
Or on the toilet'

- John Lennon

31

What unusual use do wombats have for their poo?

A: They eat it in order to retain nutrients unhelpfully filtered out.

B: They use it in mating rituals.

C: They use it to help them remember where they live.

Poo or false?

Mozart liked to make up scatological verses, including the following, which he sent to a friend: 'Oui, by the love of my skin, I shit on your nose, so it runs down your chin.'

A: Poo

B: False

33

Poo or false?

There is a pill which once ingested will make your turds appear as solid gold nuggets, which retails for £180.

A: Poo

B: False

34

Poo or false?

The shit accrued by crew on the US Navy's newest aircraft carrier will be disposed of by 'vaporising by plasma'?

A: Poo

B: False

35

Poo or false?

Some of the shooting stars we see are actually astronaut poo burning up in the atmosphere.

A: Poo

B: False

36

The 3.6 million year old Laetoli footprints, one of the most important finds concerning Human evolution and evidence of upright bipedal walking, was discovered by Paleoanthropologist Andrew Hill. But how?

A: He got stoned and while on the toilet had visions which told him where to look.

B: He found them after diving to the ground in the middle of an elephant dung fight with his colleague.

B: He discovered the right place to look having tasted some shit on the ground which proved his theory.

Why did marathon runner Paula Radcliffe poo herself during the 2005 London marathon?

A: She had stomach cramps.

B: A political protest.

C: She decided to moon an ex-boyfriend and accidentally crapped.

38

Fieldfares, a species of bird, use poo in which unusual way?

A: They inspect each other's droppings to determine who should lead the flock in formation.

B: They give droppings to their young as gifts.

C: They dive bomb predators and shit on them so that they become so covered in crap that they cannot fly.

39

Poo or false?

The phrase 'shit-eating-grin' comes from a case in Springleaf, Utah, in 1904, when a local drunk was arrested for covering his face in cat faeces and laughing hysterically during a Sunday church service.

A: Poo

B: False

40

Poo or false?

A stool transplant is a process in which a stool is taken from a healthy person and is placed in the colon of an unhealthy person suffering from IBS and other diseases. The good bacteria from the stool of healthy person then 'colonise' the digestive tract of the unhealthy one.

A: Poo

B: False

'Dance like nobody's watching. But always poo with the door closed'

- William W. Purkey

41

Poo or false?

Some species of caterpillar hurl their poo to ward off predators.

A: Poo

B: False

42

Back to Victorian London... Sanitary committees were set up in order to do what?

A: To decide which spaces stank so badly of poo and wee that they should build toilets there.

B: To ascertain which parts of the city produced the most stool.

C: To catch people using the very first public toilets for nefarious activities, after the police refused to get involved.

43

Why did a four-million-pound pile of cow manure carry on burning for days after the fire started, in Nebraska, USA?

A: It was part of a Satanist festival.

B: Using water to put it out would have contaminated the land.

C: No firefighter would agree to get close to it.

44

Chronic constipation currently affects 10% of the world's population, but is it:

A: On the rise

B: Falling

C: Staying the same

Poo or false?

The musician Screamin' Jay Hawkins honoured the troubles surrounding the constipation issue with his notorious song 'Constipation Blues.'

A: Poo

B: False

46

(Part 1) Before public sewers were invented in England, poo would be carried away on carts under cover of night, sparing residents from the smell and sight. But was the term used for the stool that was carried away?

A: Nocturnal Nuggets

B: Dark splatter

C: Night Soil

(Part 2) What happened to the poo once it had been removed?

A: It was dumped in rivers.

B: It was buried in a huge pit on the outskirts of each town, known as the crappery.

C: It was used in building materials.

48

What unusual behaviour do vultures engage in when it comes to poo?

A: They crap on their feet, the bacteria helping to kill all of bugs in their food when they land on it.

B: They dip their wing tips in poo and touch wings together mid-flight, for reasons unknown.

C: They poo a dropping for every mouthful of food they eat.

49

People fart on average how many times?

A: 1 to 2 times daily.

B: 4 to 5 times daily.

C: 7 to 8 times daily.

50

Poo or false?

The viceroy and white admiral caterpillars disguise themselves to look like poo in order to fool predators.

A: Poo

B: False

'That poo which does not kill us makes us stronger'

- Friedrich Nietzsche

51

In 2013, the games company Cards Against Humanity pranked people on Black Friday, but how?

A: They sent an email to everyone on their mailing list, simply saying 'don't buy our shit on Black Friday'.

B: They posted out literal chunks of bullshit to customers.

C: They parked a bus full of shit outside Amazon's New York headquarters.

52

Poo or false?

Beethoven was once summoned to court for drunkenly calling a local priest a 'shithead' after he refused to allow him into church to use the toilet.

A: Poo

B: False

53

Poo or false?

Not only did Lady Godiva ride naked into Coventry in protest at her husband's unfair taxation, she also picked up the horse's dung and hurled it at her husband's window.

A: Poo

B: False

54

Poo or false?

England footballer Gary Lineker once shat his pants and had to wipe his bottom along the grass to clean himself in a match against Cameroon.

A: Poo

B: False

55

In 2006, Tottenham Hotspur blamed their defeat to West Ham (meaning bitter rivals Arsenal finished above them) on what?

A: Prank poos in the dressing room, left by the Arsenal-supporting groundsman.

B: A dodgy lasagne eaten the night before which gave them stomach upsets.

C: A continuous barrage of chants calling them shit from their own disgruntled fans.

56

Because Elephant poo is **45%** fibre, it is very versatile. But what did the Thai Elephant Conservation Center in Northern Thailand discover they could make with it?

A: Footballs.

B: Notepads.

C: Model replicas of elephants.

57

What unusual use have scientists found for llama poo?

A: Cleaning drinking water.

B: In rocket fuel.

C: In anti-climb paint.

58

In 1862, every gray bat cave in the south of the United States was cleared of bat poo. But why?

A: Its explosive properties were utilised in the civil war.

B: The caves were used to stockpile food for the neighbouring towns.

C: Nobody knows! Mystery poo collectors cleaned them under cover of darkness.

59

Poo or false?

The phrase 'up shit creek without a paddle' was reportedly invented by Swedish-American actress Greta Garbo.

A: Poo

B: False

60

Poo or false?

Food only makes up a certain percentage of what you poo. If you were stop eating you would continue to poo.

A: Poo

B: False

'Don't walk in front of me; I may not follow. Don't walk behind me; I have pooed myself'

- Albert Camus

61

American football player Larry Izzo confided in his teammates at the end of a game that he'd taken a poo on the sidelines during the game without anyone noticing. How did they react?

A: They insisted he be banned for three games.

B: They made him eat a part of his boot.

C: They awarded him the match ball.

62

Scientists in China found that, like elephants, panda poo could be recycled. But what did they use it to help make?

A: Toilet paper.

B: Weights for dart flights.

C: Chopping boards.

63

Gastroenterologist Urvish Shah described an unusual occurrence he'd heard of during a colonoscopy, but what was it?

A: A patient woke up after the operation and was only able to communicate by making 'fart' noises.

B: The instrument used to remove a cyst sparked and caused a a brief flame to burn inside the patient's colon.

C: The doctor found twelve identical models of Yoda from *Star Wars* in the patient's colon.

64

Doctors in America desperate to treat a six-year-old girl who was obsessed with playing with her own faeces managed to solve the problem by doing what:

A: They created fake poo with flour, water, and food colouring.

B: One of them dressed up as a Santa Clause-esque giant poo and explained the dangers of playing with poo.

C: They asked the inventor of Barbie to come and explain why it was a bad thing.

65

In 2014, scientists invented a machine that turns poo into drinking water, but which celebrity did they invite to come in and test it?

A: Bill Gates.

B: Donald Trump.

C: Johnny Knoxville from *Jackass*.

66

What are coprolites?

A: Fossilised turds occasionally found in dinosaurs' colons.

B: Miniature particles of poo found at crime scenes that police use to track victims.

C: Slang term used for new recruits by the Boston police force.

67

Which of these shit-hot authors died on the toilet?

A: Tennessee Williams.

B: Evelyn Waugh.

C: Ian Fleming.

68

The tambaqui, a species of fish found in the Amazon, provide a pleasant service with their poo, but what is it?

A: Seeds they eat come out in their poo and are carried off downstream, eventually planting themselves to create spectacular greenery.

B: The mohilo water rat hides in the poo to keep cool.

C: The frento bat uses the poo for its nest.

69

Poo or false?

In the original lyrics to Taxman, John Lennon wrote, 'Look where you shat man, yeah you're the taxman.'

A: Poo

B: False

70

Poo or false?

In the 19th Century, New Yorkers began to buy automobiles at an increased rate because they were seen as the 'green option', due to the horse manure that was currently filling the streets.

A: Poo

B: False

'Do one thing a day that scares you. But never have a vindaloo before you fly RyanAir because it'll just be chaos'

- Eleanor Roosevelt

71

Poo or False?

The Adélie penguin can 'projectile poo' as far as a meter?

A: Poo

B: False

72

Which of these are real cockney rhyming slang for words for poo?

A: Tom Tit, Four by Two, Top Ten Hit.

B: Pony and Trap, Betty Boo, Richard the Third.

C: Or all of the above.

73

Poo or false?

Nightingale poo has made it into many a posh skin cream as a vital ingredient.

A: Poo

B: False

74

Poor or false?

And what about lipstick? Some lipsticks contain bat poo:

A: Poo

B: False

75

Apart from the obvious . . . what problems do zoos often have with their pandas?

A: They often smear their own poo on the enclosure walls, marking territory.

B: The shear quantities of food they eat means they can poo up to 20kgs a day.

C: They find it hard to digest medicines, so zookeepers have to sort through their poo to find the pills.

76

The capybara, a mammal native to South America, has an unusual pooing system. But what is it?

A: They never actually poo.

B: They poo with practically every step they take.

C: They poo twice – green and brown – and eat the former, because it retains nutrients.

77

Poo or false?

The South Asian ricefield rat has been known to balance its poo on its back and carry it over forty miles, for no apparent reason.

A: Poo

B: False

78

Poo or false?

The Masai Ostrich will build 'snow balls' of its own dung and kick them at potential mates to (somehow!) attract them.

A: Poo

B: False

79

Poo or false?

Horse stallions will often poo in big 'pillars' as a way of marking their territory.

A: Poo

B: False

80

Poo or false?

Architects have been forced in recent years to take pigeon poo into account, having to make sure that they account for the weight of the stuff on the top of buildings they're designing.

A: Poo

B: False

'Choose a job you love, and you will never have to work a day in your life. Anyway, I'm off for a poo'

- Confucius

81

Cats will often poo outside of their litter trays, but why is it?

A: A show of dominance, that they don't need to go where you tell them.

B: They're sick, and want to let you know.

C: It can be either.

82

How do bees produce honey?

A: It's 'pooed' out of a separate back passage.

B: It's 'vomited' up out of a separate stomach sack.

83

In 2010, a Scandanavian study concluded the 'normal' range for pooing times as what?

A: Between twice a day and twice a week.

B: Between three times a day and three times a week.

C: Between four times a day and four times a week.

84

In 1961, a doctor felt moved to write about how impressive the anus and rectum are in the American Journal of Proctology. But how did he praise the anal sphincter's ability to distinguish between farts and poos, allowing us to do each independently?

A: '[it is] an unparalleled act of greatness, one that even makes one doubt evolution.'

B: '[it is] unknowable to science – something to be entirely in awe of.'

C: '[it is] the protector of our dignity, yet so ready to come to our relief.'

85

Poo or false?

Around three billion people on the planet still rely on burning dung to help cook.

A: Poo

B: False

86

A woman in Ann Arbor, Michigan, is recorded as doing the longest poo in the world at a whopping 26 feet. But was *particularly* unusual about it?

A: It never happened. She is an artist who used the lie as part of an avant-garde art exhibition.

B: It was only half a centremetre wide in length.

C: It contained a piece of sweetcorn every two metres.

87

What is unusual about sperm whale poo?

A: The whales shoot it out in an aggressive form of defence.

B: It carries nutrients which help feed phytoplankton.

C: Both are true.

88

Poo or false?

A species of owl native to South America died out because it relied on the poo of an extinct species of monkey in order to build its nest.

A: Poo

B: False

In 2016, *Breaking Bad* star Bryan Cranston gave his wife a delightful poo-themed present to celebrate their 27th wedding anniversary. But what was it?

A: A sign for the bathroom door that says 'I am the one who plops'.

B: A plastic 'squatty potty', which supposedly guarantees a healthier poo.

C: A photograph of co-star Aaron Paul mid-poo.

90

The aforementioned 'squatty potty' was invented by whom?

A: Jay-Z.

B: James Crapper – a direct descendent of Thomas Crapper.

C: A Mormon from Utah who'd struggled with constipation all her life.

'Tis better to have loved and lost than to have shat yourself on the Bakerloo line in rush hour'

- Alfred Tennyson

91

What treatise on etiquette was discovered from the late 16th century?

A: One that told off wealthy citizens for showing off their rags that they used to wipe their bottoms.

B: One that demanded a distance of at least forty feet between men and women who wanted to defecate.

C: One that insisted everyone in England went for poos at 1pm every day, to consolidate the smell.

92

How quickly do turds make their way out of our bodies?

A: One to two centimetres per second.

B: Three to four centimetres per second.

C: Five to six centimetres per second.

93

Poo or false?

W.G. Grace, the legendary England cricketer, once shat on an opponent's bat, and left it in the pavilion, after he had slandered Grace's wife.

A: Poo

B: False

94

An American, George Frandsen, holds the record for collecting the most ... what?

A: Fossilized lumps of faeces.

B: Dodo droppings.

C: Model poos in the shape of Osama Bin Laden.

(Part one) Poo or false?

There is a part of the back passage the medical community named 'the anal crypt'.

A: Poo

B: False

96

(Part two) Poo or false?

There is a part of the back passage the medical community named 'the valves of Houston'.

A: Poo

B: False

(Part three) Poo or false?

There is a part of the back passage the medical community named 'Satan's slant'

A: Poo

B: False

98

In her bestselling book *Gut*, how did Giulia Enders describe the act of pooing?

A: 'More beautiful than any Shakespeare verse.'

B: 'An extraordinary thing – unmatched in nature for its sheer glory.'

C: 'A masterful performance'

99

In 1997, scientists produced an official list of examples of the various shapes and sizes of poo that the human body produces. What did they call it?

A: The Dunstable Dung Chart.

B: Bristol Stool Scale.

C: The Farnborough Faecal Map.

100

Poo or false?

In 2011, Wells police force were left with 'nothing to go on', after crafty crooks stole their station toilet.

A: Poo

B: False

ANSWERS

Did a shit job? It's time to find out...

1. A	16. B	31. C
2. B	17. C	32. A
3. A	18. A	33. A
4. B	19. A	34. A
5. B	20. A	35. A
6. A	21. A	36. B
7. C	22. A	37. A
8. A	23. A	38. C
9. B	24. A	39. B
10. A	25. A	40. A
11. B	26. B	41. A
12. A	27. C	42. A
13. B	28. A	43. B
14. B	29. C	44. A
15. B	30. C	45. A

ANSWERS

46. C	61. C	76. C	91. A
47. A	62. A	77. B	92. A
48. A	63. B	78. B	93. B
49. C	64. A	79. A	94. A
50. A	65. A	80. A	95. A
51. B	66. A	81. C	96. A
52. B	67. B	82. B	97. B
53. B	68. A	83. B	98. C
54. A	69. B	84. C	99. B
55. B	70. A	85. A	100. B
56. B	71. C	86. A	
57. A	72. C	87. C	
58. A	73. A	88. B	
59. B	74. A	89. B	
60. A	75. B	90. C	

NOTES

NOTES

NOTES